DEADLY ! CREATURES

SMALL AND DEADLY ANIMALS

T0021511

ANITA GANERI

PowerKiDS press

New York

Published in 2022 by The Rosen Publishing Group, Inc.
29 East 21st Street, New York, NY 10010

Originally Published in English by Haynes Publishing under the title:
Deadly Creatures Pocket Manual © Haynes Publishing 2019

Cataloging-in-Publication Data
Names: Ganeri, Anita, 1961-.
Title: Small and deadly animals / Anita Ganeri.
Description: New York : PowerKids Press, 2022. | Series: Deadly creatures
Identifiers: ISBN 9781725331839 (pbk.) | ISBN 9781725331853 (library bound) | ISBN 9781725331846 (6 pack) | ISBN 9781725331860 (ebook)
Subjects: LCSH: Dangerous animals--Juvenile literature.
Classification: LCC QL100.G35 2022 | DDC 591.6'5--dc23

Design: Richard Parsons

Photo Credits: Cover Dirk Ercken/Shutterstock.com; pp. 5, 6 iStock; p. 9 YUSRAN ABDUL RAHMAN/Shutterstock.com; p. 11 https://commons.wikimedia.org/wiki/File:Winged_bulldog_ant_(Myrmecia)_in_Kialla,_Australia_-_20100312.jpg; pp. 13, 15, 30, 31 Alamy; p. 17 Oceanwide Images; p. 19 feathercollector/Shutterstock.com; p. 23 https://commons.wikimedia.org/wiki/File:Mosquito_Tasmania_crop.jpg; p. 25 https://commons.wikimedia.org/wiki/File:2009-03-29Dendrobates_auratus110.jpg; p. 26 https://commons.wikimedia.org/wiki/File:Goldenergiftfrosch1cele4.jpg#mw-jump-to-license; p. 27 https://en.wikipedia.org/wiki/File:Schrecklicherpfeilgiftfrosch-01.jpg.

Manufactured in the United States of America

CPSIA Compliance Information: Batch #CSPK22. For Further Information contact Rosen Publishing, New York, New York at 1-800-237-9932.

Find us on

CONTENTS

LATRODECTUS SP.
BLACK WIDOW SPIDER

There are around 30 species of black widow spider that live in many warm places around the world, and they have a fearsome reputation. Female black widows are some of the most venomous spiders in the world. These spiders are especially common in North America and sometimes live close to towns and cities.

! VITAL STATISTICS

BODY LENGTH:	up to 0.4 inch (10 mm)
WEIGHT:	about 0.03 oz (1 g)
EATS:	insects, other spiders
LIFE SPAN:	females: up to 3 years males: up to 2 months
HABITAT:	woodlands, urban areas
DISTRIBUTION:	

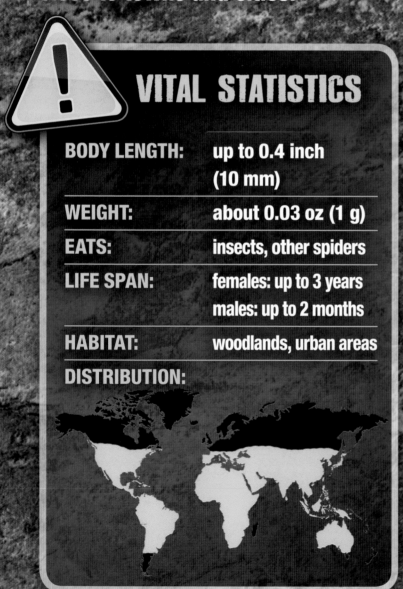

LYING IN WAIT

The black widow spider lives alone and makes its web close to the ground or under ledges, plants, or rocks. It often puts this tunnel-like web in dark spaces and spends the daytime hiding inside, lying in wait. The spider's prey crawls into the inviting dark hole and then the black widow strikes. When it sees prey on its web, the spider uses special bristles on its legs to cover its victim in sticky silk.

DID YOU KNOW?

Female black widows are famous for eating male spiders after they have mated. In reality, this does not happen very often. Male black widows are much smaller and often have markings on their backs.

SPIDER EGGS

After mating, a female spider lays up to 750 eggs in little bunches. Each bunch is laid inside a paperlike egg sac and hung on the web to protect it from predators.

DINNERTIME

Once its prey is trapped in the web, the black widow spider bites its victim and injects it with venom. The spider then drags its dead victim into a safe part of the web to eat. The black widow chews its prey and fills it with special juices from its fangs. These juices, called enzymes, turn its prey's body to mush, which the spider then sucks up. The black widow mainly eats insects and other bugs, but will also sometimes eat small mice and lizards.

DID YOU KNOW?

Many female black widow spiders have a shiny black body with a red marking shaped like an hourglass on their underside. This bright marking warns predators that the spider is venomous.

DEADLY FEATURES

The black widow spider has venom around 15 times more powerful than a rattlesnake. Although a black widow bite is not normally fatal for humans, it can kill many animals.

HAPALOCHLAENA SP.
BLUE-RINGED OCTOPUS

Compared to many other octopuses, the blue-ringed octopus is tiny. Measuring up to 7.8 inches (20 cm) across, it can easily sit on your hand. Yet it is one of the deadliest creatures in the sea, capable of killing a human with its venomous bite.

VITAL STATISTICS

BODY LENGTH:	up to 7.8 inches (20 cm)
WEIGHT:	0.3– 3.5 oz (10–100 g)
EATS:	crabs, shrimp, fish
LIFE SPAN:	unknown
HABITAT:	tidal rock pools
DISTRIBUTION:	

OCTOPUS LIFESTYLE

The blue-ringed octopus lives in rock pools along the coast around Australia and in the western Pacific region. It is easy to recognize by the blue and black rings on its yellow body. The octopus is shy, hiding away in cracks and holes. It will only attack humans if it is stepped on or picked up. Its usual prey is small crabs, shrimp, and sometimes fish.

DID YOU KNOW?

The blue-ringed octopus can change color to blend in with its surroundings. Its brightly colored rings show up only when it is alarmed or provoked.

DEADLY FEATURES

A blue-ringed octopus's poison paralyzes its victim so it cannot breathe. The venom can kill a human in 10 to 20 minutes. There is no antivenom available. At the first sign of having been bitten, get to a hospital fast!

MYRMECIA
BULLDOG ANT

There are many different species of bulldog ant, and they are also known as bull ants or jumper ants. These large ants can grow to be more than 1.6 inches (40 mm) long, and are famous for their aggressive behavior and painful stings. All species of bulldog ants only live in Australia.

VITAL STATISTICS

BODY LENGTH:	0.6–1.6 inches (15–40 mm)
WEIGHT:	unknown
EATS:	small insects
LIFE SPAN:	up to 10 weeks
HABITAT:	forests, heathland, urban areas

DISTRIBUTION:

ANT AGGRESSION

The bulldog ant can be red, orange, or black. It is so strong that it can carry prey that is seven times heavier than it is. The ant uses its powerful eyesight to track down prey. It seizes a victim in its jaws and injects venom from its stinger to kill it. The ants guard their nests fiercely and will attack anything that comes too close.

DID YOU KNOW?

Some bulldog ants are called jumper ants because they jump at anything that threatens them. They have especially strong back legs that allow them to do this.

DEADLY FEATURES

The bulldog ant's main weapons are its crushing jaws and venomous sting. Its sting can be very painful to humans, but is usually only deadly if the victim is allergic to it.

ANDROCTONUS AUSTRALIS
FAT-TAILED SCORPION

The deadly fat-tailed scorpion lives in the deserts of the Middle East and Africa. It gets its name from its wide tail. These medium-sized scorpions can be brown, black, or yellow. Like all scorpions, they have pincers at the front and a curved tail, ending in a stinger, at the back.

VITAL STATISTICS

BODY LENGTH:	4 inches (10 cm)
WEIGHT:	unknown
EATS:	insects, spiders, lizards
LIFE SPAN:	unknown
HABITAT:	deserts
DISTRIBUTION:	

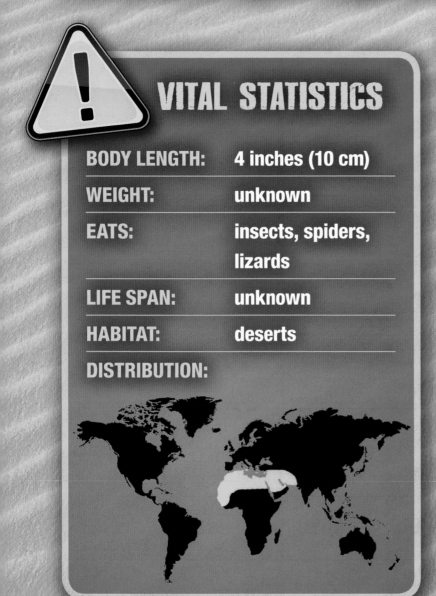

DESERT HUNTER

Fat-tailed scorpions are nocturnal. During the day, they shelter from the desert heat in burrows and cracks in the rocks. At night, they come out to hunt their prey of insects, spiders and small lizards. A scorpion waits for prey to pass by, then grabs it in its pincers. Then it curls its tail over and gives its victim a poisonous sting. It also stings to defend itself against predators, such as owls, bats, and large lizards.

DID YOU KNOW?

Baby scorpions climb onto their mothers' backs and ride piggyback for about a week until they are old enough to look after themselves.

DEADLY FEATURES

A fat-tailed scorpion's poison is deadly, and scorpion stings cause several human deaths each year. A scorpion can regulate how much poison it injects in a sting. If its whole supply is used up, it can take several days to make more.

ATRAX ROBUSTUS
FUNNEL-WEB SPIDER

Found in Australia, the Sydney funnel-web spider is one of the deadliest spiders on Earth. There are several different types of funnel-web, the most dangerous being the Sydney funnel-web. It tends to live under rocks and fallen logs, but it also likes to wander into houses and lurk in gardens and compost heaps.

VITAL STATISTICS

BODY LENGTH:	1–1.4 inches (2.5–3.5 cm)
WEIGHT:	unknown
EATS:	insects, frogs
LIFE SPAN:	8 or more years
HABITAT:	forests, gardens
DISTRIBUTION:	

FUNNEL WEBS

As their name suggests, funnel-web spiders build funnel-shaped webs. In yards, webs may be found in rock gardens and sometimes lawns. A web will be about a foot (30 cm) long and lined with silk. Silk tripwires stretch from the entrance. These warn the spiders of passing prey, mates, or danger. At night, the spider sits just inside the entrance with its front legs on the trip wires.

DID YOU KNOW?

Funnel-web spiders like to burrow in damp places because their bodies can easily dry out. But their burrows can flood if there is heavy rain.

WANDERING MALES

In the summer, male funnel-web spiders search for a mate. They seem to be attracted to water and sometimes fall into swimming pools. They can survive for up to 24 hours by trapping air around their body.

More than 40 species of funnel-web spiders live in Australia.

SPIDER APPEARANCE

Funnel-webs are medium-sized spiders, with glossy, bluish-black bodies covered in fine, velvety hairs. Female spiders grow up to 1.4 inches (3.5 cm) long (not including their legs). Males are smaller and grow up to about an inch (2.5 cm) long. Funnel-webs eat other spiders, snails, and sometimes frogs. They bite their prey to inject their poison and drag it down into the funnel to eat.

DID YOU KNOW?

A few types of funnel-web spiders live in trees. They build their webs inside rotting tree trunks and feed on beetles and other insects.

DEADLY FEATURES

Sydney funnel-webs have large fangs that are sharp enough to bite through shoes or even human fingernails. They can be extremely aggressive and will readily bite if threatened. It is the male spider that has particularly toxic venom.

HOODED PITOHUI

There are at least three poisonous species of pitohui (pih-TOH-oo-ee), which are small, brightly colored birds that live on the island of New Guinea. The hooded pitohui has a bright red or orange front and a black head. The variable and rusty pitohui are also brightly colored. This is not just for show—it is intended as a warning.

VITAL STATISTICS

BODY LENGTH:	9 inches (23 cm)
WEIGHT:	unknown
EATS:	insects, spiders
LIFE SPAN:	unknown
HABITAT:	forests, woodlands

DISTRIBUTION:

PITOHUI POISON

The pitohui is the only poisonous bird in the world. Of the three known poisonous species, the hooded pitohui is the most toxic. They all have poisonous skin and feathers. It is thought that the poison protects the birds from parasites, such as lice, and from predators, such as snakes and birds of prey.

DID YOU KNOW?

Pitohuis are nicknamed "garbage birds" because their poison means that they are not good to eat.

The pitohui's poison is similar to that found in the skin of the poison dart frog. The pitohuis do not make the poison themselves, but most likely get it from the beetles they eat. In humans, the poison can cause numbness of the skin.

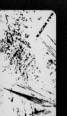

APIS MELLIFERA SCUTELLATA LEPELETIER
KILLER BEE

"Killer" bee is the name given to the Africanized bee. It came about when beekeepers in Brazil tried to breed African bees to produce extra honey. Some of the African bees were accidently released into the wild. They bred with local European bees and created a new type of "killer" bee.

VITAL STATISTICS

BODY LENGTH:	nearly 0.7 inch (2 cm)
WEIGHT:	0.003 oz (0.1 g)
EATS:	nectar and pollen
LIFE SPAN:	queen bees can live up to 2 years
HABITAT:	nests in many places
DISTRIBUTION:	

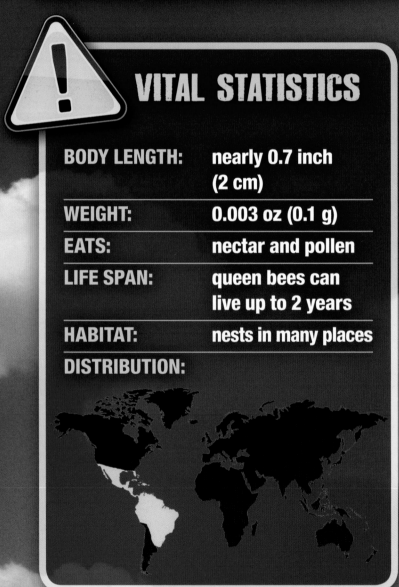

KILLER SWARMS

These bees are found in South, Central, and the southern part of North America. They are deadly because they defend their nests fiercely against anything they see as a threat, forming swarms and stinging. People disturbing their nests or loud noises can trigger this defensive reaction.

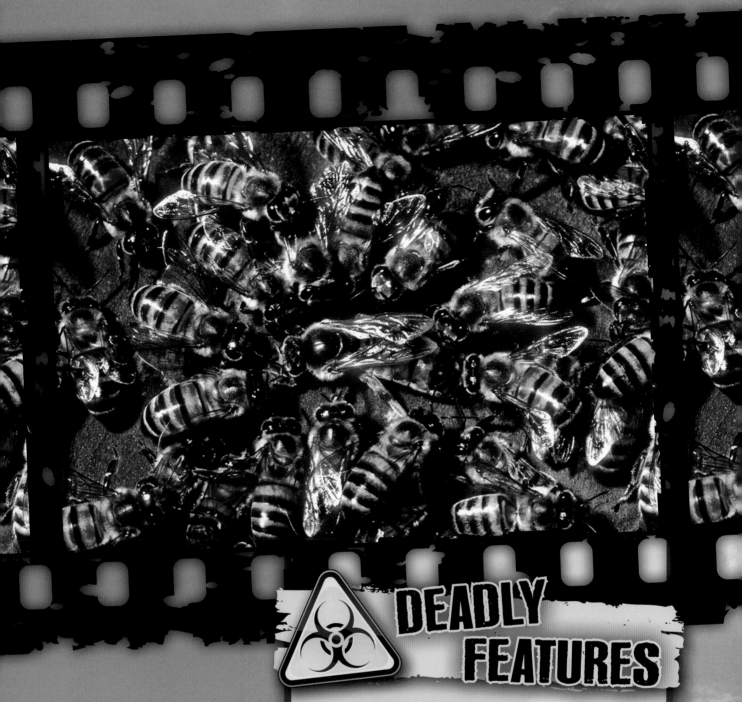

DEADLY FEATURES

DID YOU KNOW?

"Killer" bees are slightly smaller than European honeybees. Soldier bees respond to any disturbance and alert the colony to defend the nest.

The "killer" bee's sting is no stronger than a honeybee's sting, which can be painful but not dangerous. However, because killer bees attack in a swarm, many stings can occur. They will also follow a victim over a long distance.

CULICIDAE
MOSQUITO

There are more than 3,000 types of mosquito found worldwide. Despite their size, some types are deadly to humans, causing more deaths in Africa than any other creature. Most of these deaths are caused by malaria, a disease spread when an *Anopheles* mosquito bites.

VITAL STATISTICS

BODY LENGTH:	0.1–0.8 inch (3–20 mm)
WEIGHT:	2.5 mg
EATS:	blood, nectar
LIFE SPAN:	up to 6 months
HABITAT:	freshwater in warm climates

DISTRIBUTION:

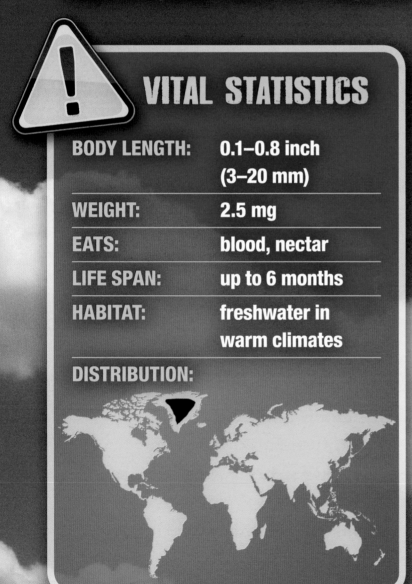

BLOODSUCKERS

Mosquitoes breed in shallow water. Although notorious for feeding on blood, their main source of food is nectar. Only females feed on blood, which is an important source of protein and iron for their eggs. They feed mainly at dawn and dusk. As the mosquito bites, it pricks two tubes into the victim's skin. One sucks up blood and the other produces saliva to keep the blood from clotting so that it will flow until the mosquito is full. It is the saliva that transmits diseases to humans.

DID YOU KNOW?

Malaria is not the only disease spread by mosquitoes. Different species can spread a variety of diseases such as encephalitis, elephantiasis, yellow fever, and the West Nile virus.

DEADLY FEATURES

The mosquito's special senses help it to find its victims by locating movement, breathing, and sweat. The different types of mosquito have caused the deaths of millions of humans worldwide.

DENDROBATIDAE
POISON DART FROG

Poison dart frogs are a group of frogs that live in the tropical rain forests of Central and South America. Most species are tiny but deadly, thanks to the poison they carry in their brightly colored skins. There are around 200 different species of poison dart frogs.

VITAL STATISTICS

BODY LENGTH:	0.6–1.6 inches (1.5–4 cm)
WEIGHT:	0.07–0.25 oz (2–7 g)
EATS:	ants, beetles, other insects
LIFE SPAN:	7–10 years
HABITAT:	rain forests
DISTRIBUTION:	

WARNING COLORS

Poison dart frogs come in a range of bright colors, including red, green, blue, and golden. Their colors make them easy to spot as they search for their insect prey during the day. But their striking colors are not simply for decoration. They are a warning to possible predators that the frogs are highly poisonous and should be left alone.

DID YOU KNOW?

Poison dart frogs get their name because poison from their skin is used by local people to tip their blow darts for hunting monkeys, jaguars, and birds.

WATER BABIES

Poison dart frogs lay their eggs in damp places on leaves, plants, and roots. When the tadpoles hatch, some parents carry them on their backs to water, where they can grow into frogs.

GOLDEN FROG (*Phyllobates terribilis*)

The golden poison dart frog lives in a tiny patch of rain forest in Colombia. It is one of the largest and deadliest of the poison dart frogs. In fact, it is thought to be one of the most poisonous land animals. Adults have a bright, golden color with dark spots. They live on the rain forest floor, often close to streams, but also have sticky pads on their feet for climbing trees. They feed on insects, which they catch with their long, sticky tongues.

ENDANGERED · SPECIES ·

DEADLY FEATURES

DID YOU KNOW?

The golden poison dart frog is deadly to most animals. But one rain forest snake can eat the frogs, although it is not totally safe from being harmed.

The golden poison dart frog stores its poison in special glands scattered across its skin. A single frog contains enough poison to kill up to 20 adult humans or 10,000 mice. Its poison works quickly, attacking the nerves and muscles and causing heart failure.

DESMODUS ROTUNDUS
VAMPIRE BAT

Vampire bats live in Central and South America and, due to their portrayal in films, are one of the most misunderstood animals. They live in colonies that normally include up to 100 bats, although colonies of 5,000 have been reported. At night, they search for prey, such as cattle, horses, and occasionally humans.

VITAL STATISTICS

BODY LENGTH:	up to 3.5 inches (9 cm)
WEIGHT:	up to 1.8 oz (50 g)
EATS:	blood of animals
LIFE SPAN:	up to 12 years
HABITAT:	caves, tree hollows
DISTRIBUTION:	

CREEPY CRAWLY

A vampire bat can also hop and jump to reach prey that is much larger than itself. It is very important that the bat's victim does not wake, as the bat is so small that it would have trouble defending itself if attacked.

DID YOU KNOW?

Vampire bats almost never kill their victims, but they occasionally carry and spread deadly infections and diseases, such as rabies, when they bite other animals.

DAYTIME REST

During the day, vampire bats sleep in darkness, hanging upside down from their roosts in the roofs of caves. In the deep of night, they wake up and go out hunting.

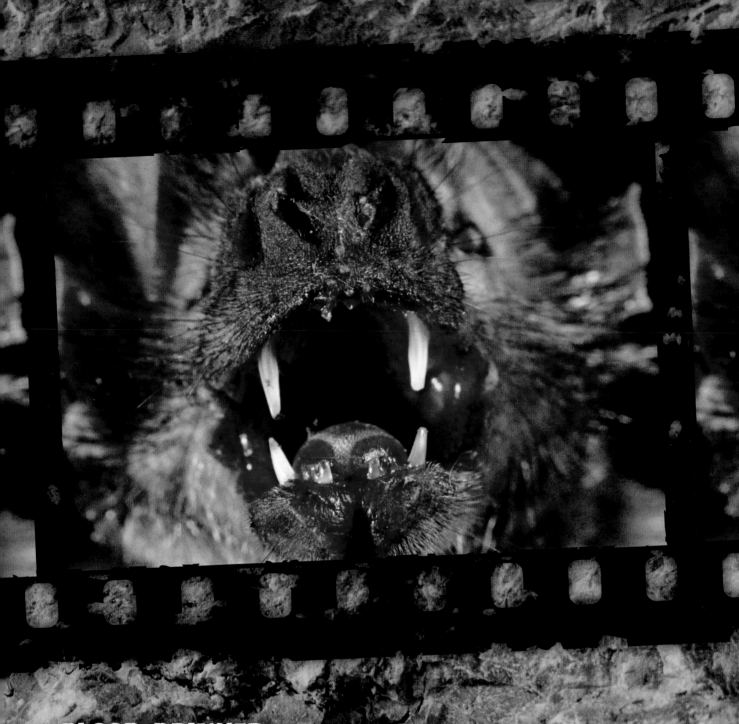

BLOOD DRINKER

When the vampire bat has found its victim and climbed on, it prepares to feed. It flattens any hairs in the way by licking the skin. Then it uses its sharp front teeth to make a small cut in the skin and uses its tongue to lap up the blood. The bat's saliva stops the blood from clotting so that it keeps flowing until the bat is full.

DID YOU KNOW?

When a vampire bat has had a big meal of blood, it can be too heavy to take off and fly away. It jumps to get itself off the ground and launch itself into flight.

DEADLY FEATURES

A vampire bat detects its prey through echolocation, smell, and sound. When it has found a suitable host, it uses special heat sensors on its nose to detect the best place to feed. The bats' teeth are so small that the victim does not feel a thing.

GLOSSARY

clotting becoming thick and partly solid

disease an illness

fangs long, sharp teeth

inject to force a liquid into something

jaws two parts of the body that open and close to hold or crush something

mate one of two animals that come together to produce babies. Also, to come together to produce babies.

poison something that can cause harm or death if taken into the body

reputation the common opinion about something

venom a poison made by an animal and used to harm or kill another animal

INDEX